9/20

FACING LIFE'S CHALLENGES

FACING SERIOUS ILLNESS

BY STEPHANIE FINNE

BLUE OWL
BOOKS

TIPS FOR CAREGIVERS

Social and emotional learning (SEL) helps children manage emotions, create and achieve goals, maintain relationships, learn how to feel empathy, and make good decisions. The SEL approach will help children establish positive habits in communication, cooperation, and decision-making. By incorporating SEL in early reading, children will be better equipped to build confidence and foster positive peer networks.

BEFORE READING

Talk to the reader about illness.

Discuss: What happens when someone is ill? How does it affect that person? How does it affect you?

AFTER READING

Talk to the reader about ways in which someone with a serious illness gets help. Explain that adults, such as doctors and nurses, work to help ill people feel better.

Discuss: Where does someone who is seriously ill find help? How do doctors and nurses help someone who is ill?

SEL GOAL

Students dealing with serious illness in their families may struggle with fear and sadness. They probably don't want to make things harder on family and friends, so they may keep their feelings inside. Help readers find a way to voice their feelings. Give them a journal to write or draw in and an open invitation to talk.

TABLE OF CONTENTS

CHAPTER 1

WHAT IS A SERIOUS ILLNESS?

Layla's grandpa has been seeing the doctor a lot. He looks thinner. Finally, his doctor tells Layla's parents the sad news. Grandpa has **cancer**.

Some people are born with a **serious illness**, like a heart **defect**. Many serious illnesses, like cancer, are **diagnosed** by a doctor. The patient isn't born with it. All serious illnesses affect the people experiencing them and their loved ones. Layla visits her grandpa in the hospital. She makes the best of her time with him.

Serious illnesses often involve many hospital visits and stays. The patient may need **medication**. Medications can help slow down the illness or make the person more comfortable.

When Eva was diagnosed, her life changed. It quickly became different from her friends' lives. She spent many months in the hospital. She lost her hair.

SIDE EFFECTS

Medications can change how someone looks. The person taking them might lose weight or their hair. Your loved one may look different. That is OK. The medications are working to help. He or she is still the same person.

CHAPTER 2

WHAT ABOUT ME?

Aiden's parents spend a lot of time caring for his brother. His family had to move to be closer to the hospital. Aiden feels bad that his brother is sick. But sometimes it feels like no one is caring for him. His life is changing, and he feels left out.

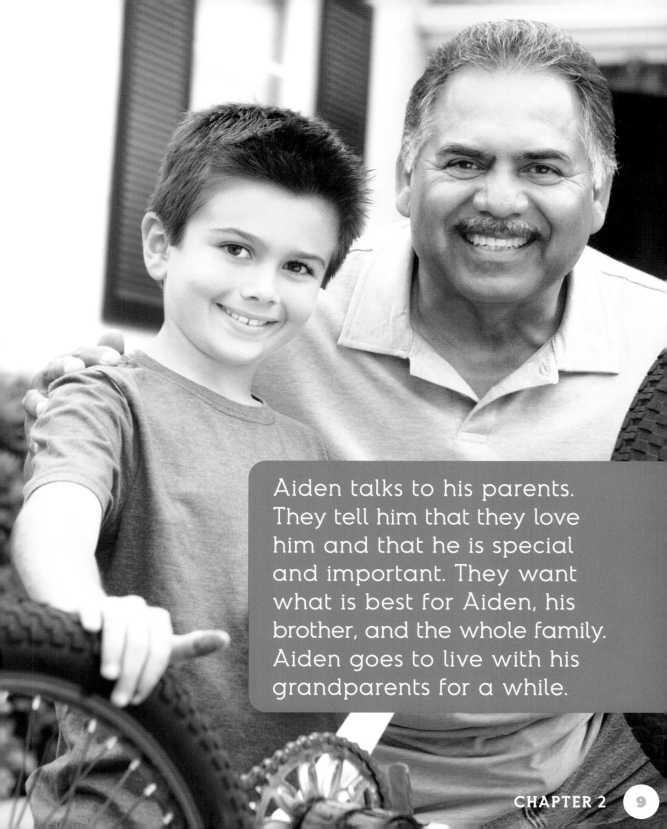

Aiden talks to his parents. They tell him that they love him and that he is special and important. They want what is best for Aiden, his brother, and the whole family. Aiden goes to live with his grandparents for a while.

You could be **jealous** of the attention your loved one needs. Or you could feel **guilty** that you can do things he or she can't.

None of these feelings are bad. But it is important to **process** them. Kayla writes and draws about her feelings. She spends time coloring.

WAYS TO PROCESS

There is no wrong way to process your feelings. Maybe you go outside or listen to music. You might want to be active and play sports. What helps you?

Watching a loved one face a serious illness can be scary. Mike is worried his uncle will die. He doesn't know what the future will be like. He is scared and confused. Could he get sick, too?

STAYING WELL

When someone you love is sick, you might worry that you will get sick, too. You can't catch most serious illnesses like you catch a cold. Your body works hard to keep you healthy! Your loved one's body is working hard, too. It just needs some help.

support group

It is normal to feel scared. Talking about his feelings helps Marcus. He is honest with his parents about his feelings.

At school, he talks to **social workers** and **counselors**. His class forms a **support** group. He talks about his feelings with his classmates. They listen to him and support him.

CHAPTER 3

WHEN A FRIEND IS SICK

Seth's classmate Mia keeps missing school. The teacher says she will be back when she is better. Seth is worried. What is wrong with Mia?

Seth visits Mia in the hospital. When Mia comes back to school, Seth invites her to play. They draw until she feels well enough to play at recess.

If you can, visit your loved one in the hospital. If you can't visit, send mail. It could be a letter or pictures you draw. You can make video calls, too! If your loved one is home, invite him or her to play. Be **patient** if he or she is tired. There are many ways to support your loved one!

Serious illnesses are hard for everyone. Try to stay positive! The doctors and nurses are working hard to help your loved one.

There are many ways you can **cope**. Even when serious illness is scary, you can stay hopeful! This will help you and your loved one.

GOALS AND TOOLS

GROW WITH GOALS

Serious illnesses are scary. It can be hard for everyone. Here are a few things to try when you are worried.

Goal: Remember that you didn't cause the illness. You may be sad. Think about what you are feeling. Identify emotions to help process them.

Goal: Start a journal. Draw or write how you are feeling each day. This will help you work through your feelings.

Goal: Learn about your body. How does it work? What is it doing to keep you from getting sick? How can you treat it well and keep it healthy?

WRITING REFLECTION

Serious illness can be scary, but practicing gratitude can help. Try it!

- Gather a journal or a piece of paper and a pencil.

- Take a deep breath in. Slowly let it out. Repeat this a few times.

- Write down the things you are grateful for. They could be your family, the doctors helping the person who is sick, or the sunshine.

- Read the list of things you are grateful for every day or any time you are feeling down.

GLOSSARY

cancer
A disease caused by cells that are not normal and spread throughout the body.

cope
To deal with something effectively.

counselors
People who are trained to help with problems or give advice.

defect
An imperfection that impairs function.

diagnosed
Determined what disease a patient has or what the cause of a problem is.

guilty
Feeling bad because you feel like you did something wrong.

jealous
Feeling unhappy or angry that someone has something you do not or that someone is loved more than you.

medication
Something, such as a pill, liquid, or lotion, that treats an illness.

patient
Able to put up with problems or delays without getting angry or upset.

process
To gain an understanding or acceptance of something.

serious illness
An illness that lasts a long time and often involves medications and hospital visits. It may be life-threatening or last the patient's whole life.

social workers
Professionals who help those who are disadvantaged and often connect them with other resources that can help.

support
Help, comfort, or encouragement.

TO LEARN MORE

FACT SURFER

Finding more information is as easy as 1, 2, 3.

1. Go to www.factsurfer.com

2. Enter "**facingseriousillness**" into the search box.

3. Choose your cover to see a list of websites.

INDEX

Blue Owl Books are published by Jump!, 5357 Penn Avenue South, Minneapolis, MN 55419, www.jumplibrary.com

Copyright © 2021 Jump! International copyright reserved in all countries. No part of this book may be reproduced in any form without written permission from the publisher.

Library of Congress Cataloging-in-Publication Data

Names: Finne, Stephanie, author.
Title: Facing serious illness / by Stephanie Finne.
Description: Minneapolis: Jump!, Inc., [2021]
Series: Facing life's challenges | Includes index.
Audience: Ages 7–10 | Audience: Grades 2–3
Identifiers: LCCN 2019058497 (print)
LCCN 2019058498 (ebook)
ISBN 9781645274162 (hardcover)
ISBN 9781645274179 (paperback)
ISBN 9781645274186 (ebook)
Subjects: LCSH: Chronic diseases—Juvenile literature. | Chronically ill—Juvenile literature.
Classification: LCC RC108 .F56 2021 (print) | LCC RC108 (ebook) | DDC 616/.044—dc23
LC record available at https://lccn.loc.gov/2019058497
LC ebook record available at https://lccn.loc.gov/2019058498

Editor: Jenna Gleisner
Designer: Jenna Casura

Photo Credits: Lightfieldstudiosprod/Dreamstime, cover; all_about_people/Shutterstock, 1; firina/iStock, 3; Photographee.eu/Shutterstock, 4; monkeybusinessimages/iStock, 5; FatCamera/iStock, 6–7; RBFried/iStock, 8; Monkey Business Images/Shutterstock, 9, 20–21; Wavebreak Media ltd/Alamy, 10–11; Hung Chung Chih/Shutterstock, 12–13 (foreground); BaanTaksinStudio/Shutterstock, 12–13 (background); SDI Productions/iStock, 14–15; andresr/iStock, 16, 17; Chernetskaya/Dreamstime, 18–19; JulieanneBirch/iStock, 18–19 (screen).

Printed in the United States of America at Corporate Graphics in North Mankato, Minnesota.